ESSENTI**AL**

Cooking

VEGETABLES

ESSENTIAL TIPS

Cooking with

VEGETABLES

Rose Elliot

DORLING KINDERSLEY

London • New York • Sydney • Moscow

A DORLING KINDERSLEY BOOK

Editor Alexa Stace
Art Editor Ann Burnham
Senior Editor Gillian Roberts
Series Art Editor Alison Donovan
Production Controller Hélène Lamassoure

Recipes for Tips 13, 14, 21, 27, 29, 31, 57, 58, 63, 73, 74, 83, 85,
92, 93, 98, 99, 100, 101 by Anne Willan: some may contain meat or fish.
Recipes for all other tips by Rose Elliot: suitable for vegetarians.

Follow either metric or imperial units throughout a recipe, never a mixture
of the two, since they are not exact equivalents.

First published in Great Britain in 1997 by
Dorling Kindersley Limited,
9 Henrietta Street, London WC2E 8PS

Visit us on the World Wide Web at http://www.dk.com

Copyright © 1997 Dorling Kindersley Limited, London

All rights reserved. No part of this publication may be reproduced, stored in a
retrieval system, or transmitted in any form or by any means, electronic,
mechanical, photocopying, recording or otherwise, without the prior written
permission of the copyright owner.

A CIP catalogue record for this book is available from the British Library

ISBN 0-7513-0477-8

Text film output by The Right Type, Great Britain
Reproduced by Colourscan, Singapore
Printed and bound by Graphicom, Italy

ESSENTIAL TIPS

101

BASIC TECHNIQUES

1 CHOOSING & BUYING VEGETABLES

Always buy vegetables that look fresh, with crisp leaves and bright colours. Avoid any with brown patches, wilted, yellowing leaves, and a limp feel. Also avoid damaged or bruised specimens. The younger the better, but "baby" ones may lack flavour.

▽ SHOOT VEGETABLES
Choose crisp stems, not withered. Asparagus tips must have tight buds.

▷ WILD MUSHROOMS
Buy in specialist stores when in season, or gather yourself, checking with an expert.

◁ CULTIVATED MUSHROOMS
Buy when plump and moist, and avoid tired-looking, wrinkled specimens.

◁ PODS & SEEDS
Beans and peas must be crisp, with a bright colour; corn moist with bright green husk.

◁ ONION FAMILY
Choose specimens that feel solid, with no sign of sprouting, or black or powdery spots. Leeks should be firm, not limp.

◁ **LEAFY GREEN VEGETABLES**
Leaves should be crisp and bright green; cabbage solid and heavy. Avoid limp, flabby leaves or brown patches.

▷ **FRUITING VEGETABLES**
Should be firm and shiny, with deep, bright colour. No brown or soft spots, or wrinkled skin.

▽ **ROOT VEGETABLES**
Buy loose, if possible, not packaged. They should be firm and heavy, not flabby or wrinkled. Any leaves attached must be fresh, not wilted.

▷ **SQUASHES & GOURDS**
Look for unbroken skin with no soft or brown patches. Winter squash should feel heavy.

◁ **TUBERS**
Tubers should be solid, with no soft spots, green or black discoloration, or sprouted eyes.

VEGETABLES FOR HEALTH
Vegetables are naturally high in vitamins and nutrients, and contain little fat and no cholesterol. For maximum nutritional benefit, eat freshly picked, in season, and do not overcook.

2 STORING VEGETABLES

Cut leaves off root vegetables and store with winter squashes, such as butternut or acorn, at cool room temperature. Store potatoes in paper sacks in a cool, dark place, to prevent them turning green. Store greens and soft vegetables, loosely wrapped, on the bottom shelf of the refrigerator or in the crisper box.

3 PEELING VEGETABLES

It is advisable to peel all vegetables unless organically grown, since pesticides concentrate in the skin, and many vegetables are also waxed to prolong their shelf life. Potatoes, aubergines, mature marrows, and squashes can be cooked without peeling, and the flesh then scooped out of the skin.

4 DICING

Diced vegetables are used as a foundation for braised dishes and casseroles, raw or cooked in soups, or as a garnish. For perfect dice, use a well-sharpened chopping knife, large or small. Grasp the knife firmly, with all your fingers wrapped around the handle, and use your other hand to steady the vegetable while you cut.

LARGE DICE ▷

SMALL DICE ▽

MEDIUM DICE △

1 Square off the sides, then cut thick or thin slices. Stack the slices and cut even strips of uniform thickness.

2 Gather the strips into a tidy pile and slice them evenly crosswise to make dice of the required size.

5 CUTTING INTO JULIENNE STRIPS

Julienne strips are matchstick-sized. They cook quickly and evenly, and so are often used in stir-fries. They are also used as a garnish. Carrots, turnips, and leeks are often cut in this way.

1 Peel the vegetable and cut a thin strip from one side so that it lies flat on the chopping board.

2 Cut crosswise into 5cm (2½in) lengths, then cut lengthwise into thin, vertical slices.

3 Stack the slices and cut them lengthwise again into strips. For very thin strips, cut again.

6 SHREDDING VEGETABLES

Leaves such as cabbage, Swiss chard, and spinach can be cut into shreds which then cook quickly and evenly. Shredded leaves can also be used as a garnish.

1 △ Separate the leaves of cabbage or lettuce, then arrange even-sized leaves together in piles. Stack the piles neatly, then roll them up tightly.

2 ◁ Hold the roll firmly with your fingers. Slice across the roll with a sharp knife to make fine or coarse shreds, depending on how you want to use them.

7 PREVENTING DISCOLORATION

For vegetables that discolour easily, such as celeriac, add 2 tbsp lemon juice or white vinegar to every litre (1¾ pints) of cold water in a bowl. Prepare the vegetables using a stainless-steel knife, and place them in the acidulated water until ready to cook.

LEMON

8 BLANCHING & REFRESHING

Vegetables are often blanched in boiling water before cooking. This softens root vegetables, and sets the colour of greens such as broccoli or spinach. Bring the water back to the boil as fast as possible after adding the vegetable, and boil for 1–2 minutes, timing from when the water reboils. To refresh green vegetables after boiling, drain, then plunge at once into cold water to set the colour, and drain again.

9 VEGETABLE PURÉES

Vegetable purées form the basis of mousses, soufflés, and sauces. They are also served as a side dish, or as a bed for fish or sliced meat. Vegetables are first boiled, baked, or steamed, then finely mashed or processed. The purée can be enriched with butter or cream, or flavoured with fresh herbs, or spices such as nutmeg, just before serving.

FOOD PROCESSOR
This produces a very fine consistency. Do not use for starchy vegetables such as potato, since they become gluey. Stringy vegetables like celery must be sieved after puréeing.

MASHER
Use a masher for starchy vegetables such as potato, which have little fibre. For large quantities, mash a bit at a time until smooth. Beat in butter, cream, or milk to lighten if you like.

FOOD MILL
This is particularly useful for vegetables with fibres or skins such as celery or peas. Force the vegetables through by turning the handle, and then sieve to remove remaining fibres.

10 TERRINE OF PEPPERS & BABY SWEETCORN

Serves 4–6

Ingredients

butter for greasing
4 tbsp grated Parmesan
3 eggs
3 tbsp single cream
salt and pepper
500g (1lb) red peppers,
grilled, peeled, and cut
lengthwise into strips
250g (8oz) baby
sweetcorn, cooked and
drained
175g (6oz) yellow peppers,
grilled, peeled, and cut
lengthwise into strips
basil sprigs, to garnish
Pesto
1 garlic clove
30g (1oz) pine nuts
30g (1oz) Parmesan
6 tbsp chopped basil
75ml (2½fl oz) olive oil

1 Preheat the oven to 150°C/300°F/gas 2. Line a 500g (1lb) loaf tin with greaseproof paper. Grease lightly and dust with 1 tbsp Parmesan.
2 Whisk the eggs, cream, and 2 tbsp Parmesan and season. Pour 3 tbsp into the tin.
3 Arrange half the red peppers in 3 thin layers, spooning a little egg mixture on each layer.
4 Arrange half the baby sweetcorn on top and spoon a little egg mixture on top.
5 Arrange the yellow peppers in 2 layers, and spoon a little egg mixture on each layer. Repeat step 4 and then step 3. Pour any remaining egg over the top and sprinkle with 1 tbsp Parmesan.
6 Bake in a bain-marie (*see below*) until firm to the touch and a skewer comes out clean, about 1¼ hours. Allow to cool before turning out.
7 Blend the pesto ingredients into a thick sauce in a food processor or blender, and season.

Serve in slices with the pesto

TERRINES

Vegetable terrines are baked slowly in a bain-marie (roasting tin half-full of water). Avoid heavy vegetables like potatoes, and vary the colours. Many vegetables give out liquid as they cook, so watery vegetables such as courgettes should be baked or sautéed first.

11 MAKING STOCK

Vegetable stock is an ideal basis for soups and stews. Place 1kg (2lb) mixed vegetables such as onions, celery, and carrots in a pan with 1.25 litres (2¼ pints) water, 2 garlic cloves, 2 bay leaves, 1 sprig thyme and 1 tbsp peppercorns. Simmer for 1 hour, then strain and cool. Use within 3 days, or freeze.

Use fresh vegetables

12 SOUPS

Vegetables are the main ingredient in many classic soups, such as minestrone, gazpacho, Scotch broth, vichyssoise, and French onion soup. Soups made with vegetables have a wonderfully fresh flavour, and are perfect for vegetarians if you use vegetable stock. Many vegetable soups are puréed after cooking, and then enriched with cream for a velvety finish.

Vegetable soup is very nutritious

13 MIXED VEGETABLE CURRY
Serves 6–8

Ingredients
75ml (2½fl oz) vegetable oil
1 cinnamon stick
6 whole cloves
1.25kg (2¾lb) potatoes, onions, and carrots, diced and kept separate
3 garlic cloves, finely chopped
1kg (2lb) cauliflower, divided into florets
500g (1lb) French beans, halved
750g (1½lb) tomatoes, skinned, deseeded, and quartered
250g (8oz) shelled peas
450ml (¾ pint) coconut milk
salt
400g (13oz) long-grain rice
Curry spice mixture
12 cardamom pods
6 dried red chillies, deseeded
3 tbsp coriander seeds
1 tbsp cumin seeds
½ tsp black mustard seeds
2 tsp fenugreek seeds
2 tsp ground turmeric
2 tsp ground ginger

VEGETABLE CURRIES
Almost all vegetables are suitable for curries: choose ones that will give a good variety of colour and texture, and be careful not to overcook them. The vegetables should be tender, but not mushy. Onions and garlic are usually added, but other favourites are okra, aubergines, peppers, and tomatoes.

1 △ To make the spice mixture, crush the cardamom pods in a mortar and extract the seeds. Put the chillies in a frying pan with the coriander and cumin seeds and dry-fry over medium heat for 2 minutes. Cool, then place in the mortar with the cardamom seeds, mustard and fenugreek seeds, and crush finely. Mix in the turmeric and ginger.

2 △ Heat the oil in a large pan, add the cinnamon stick and cloves, and cook for 30–60 seconds until fragrant. Add the onions and garlic and sauté quickly, stirring until they soften and just begin to colour. Add the curry spice mixture and cook over low heat, stirring constantly, for 2–3 minutes.

3 △ Add all the vegetables and salt to the pan and cook for 3–5 minutes, stirring to coat with the spices. Add the coconut milk; cover and simmer until the vegetables are tender, 15–20 minutes. Meanwhile, cook the basmati rice and leave covered. Remove the cinnamon stick and cloves from the curry and discard. Serve with the rice.

Serve hot with the fluffy rice

14 THAI-STYLE STIR-FRIED VEGETABLES
Serves 4

Ingredients
30g (1oz) dried Chinese mushrooms
300g (10oz) long-grain rice
60g (2oz) skinned, unsalted peanuts
1 red pepper, cored and deseeded
3 tbsp fish sauce
2 tbsp oyster sauce
1 tsp cornflour
1 stalk lemongrass, chopped
3 tbsp vegetable oil
2 garlic cloves
2 dried red chillies
500g (1lb) cauliflower, divided into florets
175g (6oz) beansprouts
500g (1lb) bok choi, shredded
175g (6oz) mangetout
3–5 sprigs of basil

2 Preheat the oven to 190°C/375°F/ gas 5. Toast the peanuts in the oven for 5–7 minutes, then chop. Slice the pepper lengthwise. Mix the fish sauce, oyster sauce, cornflour, and lemongrass in a bowl. Drain and slice mushrooms.

1 Soak the mushrooms in warm water for 30 minutes. Meanwhile, cook the rice until barely tender, 10–12 minutes. Drain the rice, spread in a buttered baking dish and cover with buttered foil. Keep warm in a very low oven after toasting the peanuts.

Fluffy white rice contrasts with the still-crisp vegetables

3 Heat the oil in a wok or frying pan. Add the garlic and chillies and stir-fry for 30 seconds. Add the cauliflower, pepper, beansprouts, and bok choi and cook for 5 minutes. Add mushrooms and mangetout and cook for 3 minutes.

4 Add the basil and sauce mixture to the wok and stir-fry for 2 minutes. Taste and season with more fish sauce and oyster sauce, if liked. Discard the chillies. To serve, spoon the rice into a ring on a serving dish and arrange the vegetables in the centre. Sprinkle with the chopped peanuts.

Arrange some pepper strips over the rice to decorate

15 STIR-FRYING

When vegetables are stir-fried, the texture remains crisp and the colour bright. The vegetables must be cut into small, uniform pieces so that they can be tossed easily and cook quickly in the high heat of the wok or pan. Slice long vegetables such as leeks and carrots diagonally, and cut short round ones in small, thin slices. Groundnut or rapeseed oil is best for stir-frying – use just enough to coat the wok or pan.

16 DEEP-FRYING

Vegetables such as potato and parsnip chips, sliced onions, broccoli florets, or courgette or aubergine sticks all deep-fry well. Most need a coating of batter for protection, although the roots and tubers do not. Use a mild-flavoured oil such as groundnut or rapeseed.

VEGETABLE OILS

17 VEGETABLE TEMPURA
Serves 4

Ingredients
1 egg
125g (4oz) plain flour,
sifted with a pinch of salt
125ml (4fl oz) tepid water
groundnut oil for frying
1 carrot, cut into thin strips
1 red onion, sliced
125g (4oz) mangetout
125g (4oz) shiitake
mushrooms, thinly sliced
Dipping sauce
1 tbsp grated ginger root
2 tbsp mirin (Japanese
sweet rice wine)
3 tbsp light soy sauce

Serve with dipping sauce

1 Mix together the ingredients for the dipping sauce and pour into individual small bowls.
2 To make the batter, break the egg into the flour and salt in a bowl and mix lightly with a fork. Add the water and stir to form a batter.
3 Pour about 8cm (3in) of oil into a large pan over high heat. When the oil reaches 180°C/350°F – or

when a cube of stale bread browns in 30 seconds – dip 3 or 4 pieces of vegetable into the batter and drop them into the oil.
4 Fry for about 1 minute on each side until crisp, then remove with a slotted spoon. Drain on kitchen paper, but do not cover.
5 Continue until all the vegetables are deep-fried. Serve at once.

18 Braising: Spiced Red Cabbage

Serves 4

Ingredients
30g (1oz) butter
1 tbsp groundnut oil
1 large onion, chopped
2 large cooking apples
750g (1½lb) red cabbage,
  cored and shredded
pinch of ground cloves
½ tsp ground cinnamon
60g (2oz) sultanas
1 tbsp soft brown sugar
1 tbsp red wine vinegar
salt and pepper
chopped chives

Braising
*Slow cooking with a
small amount of liquid in
a covered pan – braising
– is ideal for heartier
vegetables such as celery
or cabbage. The slow
cooking allows flavours
to mingle.*

1 Melt the butter with the oil in a large pan over moderate heat. Add the onion, then cover and cook gently for 5 minutes.
2 Peel, core, and chop the apples just before cooking to prevent them discolouring. Stir the apples into the pan, then cover and cook for another 3 minutes.
3 Add the cabbage to the pan and stir well to mix. Pour in about 450ml (¾ pint) cold water. Stir in the cloves, cinnamon, sultanas, sugar, and vinegar. Reduce the heat, cover, and cook until the cabbage is very tender, about 1 hour.
4 Season well and serve at once.

Variation: red cabbage with chestnuts
Omit water, cinnamon, sultanas, and sugar. Add 1 bay leaf, 1 garlic clove, crushed, ½ tsp ground nutmeg, 16–20 peeled chestnuts (fresh, canned, or frozen), and 150ml (¼ pint) each red wine and vegetable stock. Just before serving, stir in 2 tbsp redcurrant jelly and season.

*Garnish with
chopped chives*

LEAFY GREEN VEGETABLES

19 LEAFY VARIETIES

All leafy green vegetables contain vitamins C and E. They are also high in beta-carotene, a source of vitamin A. Leaves are best eaten young and tender, and lightly cooked. Cabbage, in particular, should be cooked so that it still has some texture, and is not soggy.

▷ *Broccoli can be green, purple, or white. Florets are best steamed. Cook stalks separately.*

△ *Savoy cabbage has green crinkly leaves. It is a good choice for stuffing.*

▷ *Cauliflower is best steamed until just tender, to avoid overcooking.*

◁ *Spinach should be rinsed and drained, then cooked with the water that clings to the leaves.*

◁ **Swiss chard**
*resembles spinach,
but the white stems
can be eaten as well
as the leaves.*

▽ **Red cabbage** *is
often cooked with
vinegar, apples,
and sugar.*

◁ **Kale** *comes in
curly- and smooth-
leaved varieties. All
have a pronounced,
quite strong flavour.*

20 PREPARING BROCCOLI

Choose tightly packed heads: avoid
any with drooping leaves or yellow
flowers. You can divide the heads
into small florets before cooking.

1 △ Trim the base of each floret stalk
and discard any tough leaves. Using
a small sharp knife, peel away the tough
outer skin from the base of the stalk up
to the head of the floret.

2 △ Split each stalk lengthwise several
times to divide the broccoli. Lay the
stalks on a board and cut off the florets.
Slice the stalks and cook separately as
they will take longer than the florets.

21

21 BROCCOLI & MUSHROOM QUICHE

Serves 6–8

Ingredients

250g (8oz) prepared
shortcrust pastry
500g (1lb) broccoli florets
30g (1oz) butter
2 garlic cloves, chopped
175g (6oz) mushrooms, sliced
salt and pepper
ground nutmeg
3 eggs
2 egg yolks
375ml (12fl oz) milk
250ml (8fl oz) double cream
60g (2oz) grated Parmesan

1 Preheat the oven to 220°C/425°F/gas 7. Roll out the pastry to a 30cm (12in) round and use to line a greased 25cm (10in) flan tin. Prick the base, then chill for 15 minutes. Line the shell with foil and dried beans and bake for 15 minutes. Remove foil and beans; bake 5 minutes more.

2 Trim off broccoli stalks and slice finely. Boil florets and stalks for 3–5 minutes until just tender. Drain, rinse under cold water, then drain again. Heat the butter in a frying pan. Add the garlic, mushrooms, salt, pepper, and pinch of nutmeg. Cook until all the liquid has evaporated, 5 minutes.

3 Reduce oven heat to 190°C/375°F/gas 5. Whisk the eggs, yolks, milk, cream, Parmesan, salt, pepper, and pinch of nutmeg in a bowl. Spread the mushrooms on the pastry shell. Arrange the broccoli on top. Ladle the custard over the broccoli and bake until browned and set, 30–35 minutes.

22 PREPARING CAULIFLOWER

Cauliflower can be cooked whole, in halves or quarters, or divided into small florets with stalks trimmed. If you are cooking a cauliflower whole, it is still necessary to remove the tough outer leaves, stalk, and core.

1 Cut off outer leaves and trim stalk. Cut around core to remove it.

2 If cooking as florets, divide into pieces, then cut into florets.

23 AROMATIC VEGETABLES

Serves 2 (main course) or 4 (starter)

Ingredients
2 tbsp olive oil
2 fennel bulbs, thinly sliced
1 onion, chopped
2 garlic cloves, chopped
500g (1lb) tomatoes, skinned and chopped
1 tbsp coriander seeds, crushed
½ medium cauliflower, divided into florets
125g (4oz) green beans
125g (4oz) button mushrooms, halved
salt and pepper
2–3 tbsp chopped parsley

1 Warm the oil in a large pan. Add fennel, onion, and garlic, cover and cook for 5 minutes. Stir in tomatoes and coriander seeds. Cook until vegetables are tender and liquid has evaporated, 20 minutes.
2 Meanwhile, place cauliflower and beans in a pan and pour on boiling water to 1cm (½in) deep. Cover and cook for 3–4 minutes until tender. Drain, refresh under cold water and drain thoroughly.
3 Add mushrooms to fennel and cook for 4 minutes. Add beans and cauliflower, and season. Serve warm or cold, sprinkled with parsley.

BRUSSELS SPROUTS

24 PREPARING BRUSSELS SPROUTS

Choose small, tightly closed heads with a bright green colour. Trim the base with a sharp knife and discard the outer leaves. Cut a cross in the core of each sprout to ensure even cooking. Boil or steam until just tender when tested with the point of a knife. Do not overcook or they will be soggy and tasteless.

25 PREPARING CHESTNUTS

Chestnuts are a traditional accompaniment to cabbage dishes. If using fresh chestnuts, pierce each one with the point of a small, sharp knife. Place them in a pan, cover with water and bring to the boil. Take out a few chestnuts at a time and peel while they are still hot. If difficult to peel, boil for a few minutes longer.

Peel with a sharp knife

26 HOW TO STUFF A CABBAGE

Carefully remove 10 outer leaves from a 1.4kg (3lb) Savoy cabbage. Blanch the leaves in boiling salted water for 1 minute, then place in a bowl of cold water. Drain and pat dry, then cut out the thick central rib from each leaf. Line a large bowl with a damp tea towel, then line the bowl with overlapping leaves, allowing them to extend about 5cm (2in) above the rim of the bowl. Place one leaf at the bottom of the bowl.

MOULDING THE SHAPE
Arrange leaves overlapping, stalk end up, to recreate original shape of cabbage head.

$\mathscr{27}$ CHESTNUT-STUFFED CABBAGE

Serves 6

Ingredients

1kg (2lb) fresh chestnuts, peeled (Tip 25)
Savoy cabbage heart, cored and shredded
60g (2oz) butter
125g (4oz) boned pork, cut into chunks
1 onion, chopped
2 celery sticks, thinly sliced
zest of 1 lemon
10 parsley sprigs, finely chopped
10 sage leaves, finely chopped
2 slices white bread, crumbled
salt and pepper
2 eggs, beaten

1 △ Cook the chestnuts in boiling water until tender, then drain and chop. Blanch the cabbage, drain and pat dry. Melt the butter in a frying pan, add the cabbage and cook until tender, 7–8 minutes. Transfer to a large bowl.

2 △ Finely chop the pork and onion in a food processor, then place in the frying pan with the celery and cook until the pork is browned, 5–7 minutes. Add the chestnuts, lemon zest, parsley, sage, breadcrumbs, salt and pepper to the cabbage. Add the pork mixture and mix well together. Pour in the beaten eggs and stir until well combined.

3 △ Spoon the stuffing into the lined bowl (*Tip 26*), pressing down well, then fold the leaves over. Gather the ends of the tea towel together and tie with string to make a ball. Place the ball in a large pan of boiling water, set a plate on top, and simmer for 50–60 minutes or until a skewer comes out hot. Drain. Serve with tomato sauce (*Tip 36*).

28 PREPARING SWISS CHARD

The stems of Swiss chard can be eaten as well as the leaves. Leaves and stems are cooked separately.

1 △ Trim off the root from the Swiss chard with a large sharp knife and discard any tough leaves and stems. Cut off the leaves and reserve.

2 △ Using a vegetable peeler, remove any strings from the outer sides of the stems. Cut the stems into 1cm (½in) slices.

29 SWISS CHARD CRÊPES

Serves 6

Ingredients
125g (4oz) plain flour, sifted
½ tsp salt
3 eggs
250ml (8fl oz) milk
3–4 tbsp vegetable oil
Filling
750g (1½lb) prepared Swiss chard (Tip 28)
30g (1oz) butter, plus extra for greasing
2 garlic cloves, finely chopped
3 shallots, finely chopped
90g (3oz) goat's cheese, crumbled
125g (4oz) feta cheese, crumbled
salt and pepper
Cream sauce
250ml (8fl oz) milk
30g (1oz) butter
2 tbsp plain flour
125ml (4fl oz) double cream
ground nutmeg
30g (1oz) Gruyère cheese, grated

Gruyère gives a golden top

1 △ Whisk flour, salt, eggs, and half the milk into a batter. Let stand for 30 minutes. Beat in rest of milk. Heat 1 tbsp of oil in an omelette pan. Add a small ladle of batter and swirl to coat pan. Cook until brown underneath, then turn. Turn out on a plate. Repeat to make 12 crêpes.

2 △ Blanch the chard leaves for 2–3 minutes, then drain and chop. Heat butter in a frying pan and cook garlic and shallots until soft. Add chard stems and cook until tender. Add chard leaves and cook for 2–3 minutes, then remove from heat. Add cheeses and season.

3 △ Preheat the oven to 180°C/350°F/ gas 4. To make sauce, heat milk to just boiling. Melt butter in a pan, whisk in flour and cook for 1 minute. Remove from heat and whisk in hot milk. Return to heat and whisk until thickened. Add cream and pinch of nutmeg. Simmer for 2 minutes then remove from heat.

4 △ Place 2 dessertspoons of filling on one half of a crêpe. Fold over, then fold again to form a triangle. Place in a greased baking dish and repeat until all crêpes are used, overlapping them in the dish. Spoon sauce over crêpes, sprinkle with Gruyère and bake for 20–25 minutes until brown. Serve hot.

30 COOKING SPINACH

Remove spinach stems before cooking. Rinse the leaves and place in a pan. Cover and cook over high heat until leaves wilt. Stir, cover and cook until leaves are completely wilted and tender, 1–2 minutes. Drain thoroughly before using.

Fold leaf in half and tear out stems

31 SPINACH TIMBALES

Serves 10

Ingredients
1.4kg (3lb) spinach
60g (2oz) butter, diced
250ml (8fl oz) double cream
4 eggs
2 egg yolks
pinch of ground nutmeg
pinch of cayenne pepper
salt and pepper
Butter sauce
3 tbsp white wine vinegar
3 tbsp dry white wine
2 shallots, finely chopped
250g (8oz) butter, cubed

SERVE TIMBALES UNMOULDED WITH BUTTER SAUCE

LINING THE TIMBALES
Line greased 90ml (3fl oz) moulds with the blanched leaves and drape over edge.

1 Preheat the oven to 190°C/375°F/gas 5. Blanch 30 spinach leaves for 30 seconds, then dip in iced water. Drain and use to line 10 moulds (*left*).
2 Cook remaining spinach (*Tip 30*) and chop. Melt butter in a pan. Cook spinach for 3 minutes. Add cream and leave to cool. Stir in eggs, yolks, and seasoning. Spoon into the moulds and cover with buttered foil. Place in a tin half-filled with boiling water and bake for 12–15 minutes.
3 To make the sauce, boil vinegar, wine, and shallots to a glaze. Whisk in butter gradually, bring to the boil, still whisking, then strain.

32 SPINACH ROULADE
Serves 6 as main course

Ingredients

500g (1lb) young spinach
15g (½oz) butter
4 eggs, separated
salt and pepper
ground nutmeg
4 tbsp grated Parmesan
250g (8oz) cream cheese
1 tbsp milk
1 red pepper, grilled, peeled, and
cut into strips

1 Preheat the oven to 200°C/400°F/ gas 6. Line a 36 x 24cm (14 x 10 in) Swiss roll tin with non-stick paper.
2 Cook the spinach (*Tip 30*). Work in a food processor with the butter and egg yolks until smooth. Season with salt, pepper, and nutmeg.
3 Whisk the egg whites until stiff and fold into the spinach mixture with a metal spoon. Pour into the tin and smooth the top. Sprinkle with half the Parmesan.
4 Bake for 12–15 minutes until just firm, and spongy in the centre.

Sprinkle the remaining Parmesan over a large sheet of greaseproof paper and turn out the roulade onto it. Peel off the lining paper.
5 Beat the cheese with the milk and spread evenly over the roulade. Arrange the pepper strips on top, then roll up from one of the short ends. Serve the roulade with yellow or red pepper sauce (*Tip 93*).

33 STEAMING TO PRESERVE VITAMINS

Steaming is one of the best ways of preserving the nutrients in vegetables, but be careful not to overcook. Use a metal or bamboo steamer and lay the vegetables in a single layer. Place over boiling water and cover. Cook until just tender.

LID MUST FIT SNUGLY

FRUITING VEGETABLES

34 FRUITING VARIETIES

All fruiting vegetables are rich in vitamin C. Red-skinned kinds such as tomatoes and red peppers have the most, and also contain significant amounts of beta-carotene, a valuable source of vitamin A.

◁ *Green tomatoes are just unripe red tomatoes. They can be fried or made into chutney.*

△ *Avocados add a rich, buttery flavour to soups and baked dishes.*

△ *Mild chillies can be cooked and stuffed like peppers, or added to stews.*

▷ *Plum tomatoes have a meaty flesh, ideal for soups and sauces.*

▷ *Jalapeño chillies are medium hot. They can be used to make chilli sauces.*

▽ *Green peppers are unripened red peppers. They are ideal for stuffing.*

▽ *Yellow peppers have a sweet flavour, especially when grilled and peeled.*

△ *Red peppers are sweeter than unripe green ones.*

△ *Aubergines can be large and oval or small and round.*

35 PEELING & DESEEDING TOMATOES

Tomatoes are often peeled and deseeded before being chopped so that they will cook down or process to form a smooth purée.

1 △ Cut out the core of each tomato with a paring knife, then turn over and lightly score a cross in the base.

2 △ Place the tomatoes in boiling water for a few seconds until the skins start to split. Remove immediately.

3 △ Peel off the skins when cool enough to handle. Cut the tomatoes in half crosswise and scoop out the seeds.

36 TOMATO SAUCE
Makes 300ml (½ pint)

Ingredients
1 tbsp olive oil
1 small onion, finely chopped
1 garlic clove, finely chopped
1kg (2lb) whole ripe tomatoes
sea salt

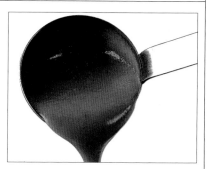

1 Warm the oil in a large pan over a moderate heat. Add the chopped onion and garlic, cover, and cook until the mixture is tender but not browned, about 4 minutes.
2 Add the tomatoes and reduce the heat. Cover and cook until the tomatoes have collapsed, about 15 minutes. Remove from the heat.
3 Purée the tomatoes in a food processor or blender. Pass through a sieve, return to the pan, and season with sea salt. Reheat gently just before serving, or serve cold.

37 PREPARING PEPPERS

The cores and seeds must always be discarded before using peppers. The peppers may be grilled and peeled before coring, or they can be cored, halved, and then grilled to char the skin. Chillies are also usually deseeded, as the seeds and core are the hottest part.

ADVICE ABOUT CHILLIES
Chillies vary from mild to searingly hot – the seeds are hotter than the flesh, so remove if in doubt. Wash hands thoroughly after preparing them.

1 ◁ With a small knife, cut around each pepper core. Twist the core and pull it out.

2 ▷ Halve the pepper and scrape out the seeds. Cut away the pith-like ribs of the core.

38 GRILLING A PEPPER

Grilling peppers intensifies the flavour, and also makes it easy to peel off the skin. Roast the pepper under a hot grill, turning until the skin is black and blistered, 10–12 minutes. Place the pepper in a plastic bag, fasten, and leave until cool. Peel off the skin with a sharp knife and rinse the pepper under cold water.

PEELING OFF THE SKIN

Filling a pepper with stuffing

39 STUFFING VEGETABLES

Many vegetables such as peppers, tomatoes, aubergines, and squash make natural containers. Usually the stuffing is baked or grilled inside the container. Avoid packing the vegetable so tightly that it bursts during cooking, and precook the container (such as halved aubergines) as necessary. The stuffing may also be cooked separately and spooned inside a precooked "container" before serving.

40 STUFFED PEPPERS
Serves 4

Ingredients
2 red & 2 yellow peppers
2 aubergines, diced
1 onion, sliced
olive oil for brushing
4 tomatoes, quartered
8 fresh basil leaves, torn in pieces
1 tbsp balsamic vinegar
salt and pepper

1 Halve and core the peppers
(Tip 37), grill, then peel (Tip 38).
2 Place the aubergine and onion in
the grill pan, brush with oil, and
grill until tender, turning from time
to time. Add the tomatoes, turn
again, and grill for 3–5 minutes.
3 Arrange the peppers in a greased
baking dish. Sprinkle the stuffing
with basil and vinegar, season,
then spoon into the peppers. Cover
with foil and reheat under the grill.

41 HERBY STUFFED TOMATOES
Serves 4

Ingredients
1 shallot, finely chopped
3 tbsp finely chopped parsley
1 tsp chopped thyme
60g (2oz) dried breadcrumbs
2 tbsp olive oil
4 beefsteak tomatoes
salt and pepper

1 Preheat the oven to 180°C/350°F/
gas 4. Mix together the shallot,
parsley, thyme, breadcrumbs, and
olive oil to make the stuffing.
2 Slice the tops off the tomatoes
and reserve. Scoop out the seeds
with a teaspoon. Stand the
tomatoes in a greased baking dish
and season the insides. Spoon in
the stuffing and replace the tops.
3 Cook the tomatoes in the oven
for about 15 minutes, until heated
through but still holding their
shape. Serve warm or cold.

42 AUBERGINE PURÉE

Prepare 3 large aubergines, brush with oil, then place under a hot grill for 20 minutes. Peel, then purée with 1 garlic clove, 3 tbsp lemon juice, sea salt, and 150ml (¼ pint) olive oil. Serve as a dip with pitta bread.

1 Cut the aubergine in half lengthwise and discard the stalk.

2 Cut around the rim, and score the flesh in a crisscross pattern.

43 STUFFED BABY AUBERGINES

Serves 4

Ingredients

6 baby aubergines, halved lengthways, stalks left on
1 tbsp olive oil
1 medium-sized onion, chopped
1 garlic clove, chopped
125g (4oz) mushrooms, chopped
2 medium tomatoes, chopped
1 tbsp chopped flat-leaf parsley
30g (1oz) pine nuts
salt and pepper

1 Preheat the oven to 180°C/350°F/gas 4.
2 Blanch the aubergines in boiling water for 3–4 minutes. Drain and cool. Scoop out the flesh, leaving the shells intact. Chop the flesh and place the shells in a greased ovenproof dish.
3 Warm the oil in a pan, add the onion, and cook for 5 minutes. Stir in the aubergine flesh, garlic, and mushrooms, and cook for 5 minutes. Remove from the heat, add the tomatoes and parsley, and season well. Spoon the filling into the aubergine shells, sprinkle with pine nuts and bake for 15 minutes.

Stuffed aubergines are delicious served hot, warm, or cold.

PODS & SEEDS

44 POD & SEED VARIETIES

These vegetables are a good source of carbohydrates and fibre, as well as being rich in beta-carotene (vitamin A) and vitamin C. Dried beans and peas (pulses) are a valuable source of protein for vegetarians.

▷ *Runner beans are best eaten young. Remove their strings before cooking.*

▷ *French beans (or haricots verts) are tender and highly flavoured, with no strings.*

◁ *Sweetcorn should be eaten very fresh, before its sugars convert to starch.*

◁ *Garden peas are best enjoyed freshly picked, and still young and tender.*

△ *Mangetout can be stir-fried or steamed for eating whole.*

▽ *Okra or ladies' fingers are used to thicken gumbos and stews.*

◁ *Broad beans, with a distinctive, earthy flavour, make robust soups and purées.*

45 SKINNING BROAD BEANS

The soft skins of young beans are tender enough to eat, but older beans have unpalatably tough skins. To remove before cooking, make a lengthwise slit in the skin. Pinch the opposite end to squeeze out the bean. To remove after cooking, simply squeeze the bean from its skin.

SQUEEZE TO REMOVE BEAN

46 TERRINE OF THREE VEGETABLES

Serves 6

Ingredients

butter for greasing
dry finely grated Parmesan
250g (8oz) carrots, chopped
250g (8oz) turnips, chopped
300g (10oz) broad beans
45g (1½oz) butter
3 tbsp single cream
3 eggs
salt and pepper
6 tbsp chopped chervil

1 Preheat the oven to 160°C/325°F/gas 3. Line a 500g (1lb) loaf tin with baking parchment. Grease lightly and dust with Parmesan.
2 Bring 3 pans of water to the boil. Cook the carrots and turnips separately until tender, 10–12 minutes, then drain. Cook the beans in the third pan until tender, 5 minutes, then drain. When cool, skin the beans (*Tip 45*).
3 Purée the carrots in a food processor with a third each of butter and cream and 1 egg. Place in a bowl and season. Repeat with the turnips and beans, keeping the purées separate.
4 Pour the carrot purée into the tin, and sprinkle evenly with half the chervil. Add the beans, then cover with the remaining chervil. Top with the turnip purée and level the surface.
5 Bake in a tin half-filled with hot water until firm to the touch and a skewer in the centre comes out clean, about 1¼ hours. Turn out when cool.

Serve the terrine with a fresh tomato sauce (Tip 36).

47 HUSKING SWEETCORN & REMOVING THE KERNELS

To husk corn, pull the papery husk down to the base and cut off. Strip off the silky threads. The kernels can then be cut whole from the cob. Hold the cob at an angle on a board and cut downwards from the tip with a sharp knife. Working over a bowl, scrape off the remaining corn pulp with the back of the knife.

Cut off whole kernels

48 CORN BREAD
Serves 8

Ingredients
2 corn cobs, husks removed
150g (5oz) polenta (fine cornmeal)
125g (4oz) strong white (bread) flour
50g (1¾oz) sugar
1 tbsp baking powder
1 tsp salt
2 eggs
60g (2oz) unsalted butter, melted,
plus extra for greasing and glazing
250ml (8fl oz) milk

1 Preheat the oven to 220°C/425°F/ gas 7. Remove the corn kernels and pulp from the cobs (*Tip 47*).
2 Sift the polenta, flour, sugar, baking powder, and salt into a large bowl and make a well in the centre. Tip the corn into the well.
3 Whisk the eggs, melted butter, and milk in a bowl to blend well.
4 Pour three-quarters of the milk into the well. Stir in gently,

gradually incorporating all the dry ingredients. Add the remaining egg mixture; stir to a smooth batter.
5 Brush a heavy frying pan with melted butter. Pour in the batter and brush the top generously with melted butter. Bake until the bread begins to shrink from the sides and a skewer tests clean, about 20–25 minutes. Cool on a wire rack, then serve warm, with butter if liked.

49 HANDLING OKRA

Okra (also called ladies' fingers) contains a sticky juice that is released if the pod is cut. When okra is sliced and cooked, this gelatinous quality helps to thicken dishes such as gumbo. To avoid the slippery texture (which some people dislike), cook the pods whole, not cut.

RAW OKRA

50 PASTA PRIMAVERA

Serves 4 as main course

Ingredients
175g (6oz) podded broad beans, fresh or frozen
30g (1oz) butter
125g (4oz) green beans
125g (4oz) mangetout
250g (8oz) pasta ribbons, such as tagliatelle
2 tbsp chopped parsley
1 tbsp chopped dill
1 tbsp chopped chives
salt and pepper

1 Cook the broad beans in boiling water until just tender, about 2 minutes. Drain, allow to cool, then pop the beans out of their skins. Place in a pan with the butter and reserve.
2 Cook the green beans in boiling water until just tender, about 3–4 minutes. Drain and add to the pan with the broad beans.
3 Blanch the mangetout in boiling water for 1 minute. Drain and add to the other vegetables. Place the pan over a gentle heat so that the vegetables warm in the melting butter.
4 Bring a large pan of salted water to the boil. Add the pasta, stir, then boil until the pasta is cooked but still firm to the bite.
5 Drain the pasta, then return to the pan. Add the vegetables and herbs, then season to taste. Toss well, so that the pasta is coated with butter and herbs.

Serve at once in warm bowls

51 GREEN PEA SOUP

Serves 4–6

Ingredients

750g (1½lb) peas in the pod
30g (1oz) butter
6 shallots, finely chopped
750ml (1¼ pints) vegetable
stock (Tip 11)
1 tsp sugar
salt and pepper
1 small round lettuce, shredded
6 sprigs of mint, shredded
125ml (4fl oz) double cream
juice of 1 lemon

1 Shell the peas into a bowl: there should be about 275g (9oz). Melt the butter in a pan, add the shallots, and cook gently, stirring occasionally, until they are soft but not brown, 2–3 minutes. Add the peas. Stir in the stock, sugar, salt, and pepper and bring to the boil. Cover and simmer until the peas are almost tender, 12–20 minutes. Add the shredded lettuce and mint leaves, reserving a little for garnish. Cover and simmer for another 5 minutes.

2 Purée the soup in a food processor or blender and return to the pan. Stir 90ml (3fl oz) of the cream into the soup (reserve the rest for decoration) and the lemon juice. Bring just to the boil and taste for seasoning. Ladle the soup into warm bowls. To decorate, drip cream from a teaspoon to form a circle of drops on the soup, then draw the tip of a small knife through the drops to create a circle of hearts. Garnish with shredded lettuce and mint.

ONION FAMILY

52 ONION VARIETIES

The onion and its many relatives are widely used for seasoning and flavouring dishes, and are also a source of vitamin E and selenium: both important antioxidant nutrients. Shallots and garlic are especially prized for their unique, pungent flavour, although garlic is sweet and mild when cooked.

▷ **White onions** are sweet, mild, and good for stuffing or braising.

△ **Spring onions** need little cooking. They are ideal to flavour stir-fries.

◁ **Shallots** give a strong, assertive onion flavour to soups, stews, stir-fries, and curries.

△ **Garlic** is at its best when fresh, young, and juicy.

▷ **Red onions** are sweet or strong depending on variety.

▽ **Yellow onions** are best used in hearty dishes such as beef stews, since they tend to be strong.

◁ **Leeks** are the mildest of the onion family. They can be served alone, with a cheese or butter sauce, or with vinaigrette.

53 CLEANING LEEKS

Leeks are often cooked whole, but all grit must be removed from between the leaves. Trim off the root and discard the coarse outer leaves. Trim the tops of the green leaves. Place each leek on a board, and make several cuts lengthwise with a sharp knife. Hold the leek upside down and swirl vigorously in a large bowl of cold water to loosen any dirt. Drain well.

Slit from the top to about halfway down.

54 LEEK PARCELS
Makes 8

Ingredients
500g (1lb) waxy potatoes, diced
350g (12oz) leeks, finely sliced
150ml (5fl oz) single cream
2 tbsp chopped parsley
salt and pepper
8 sheets of filo pastry
melted butter, for brushing

1 Cook the potatoes and leeks separately in boiling water until just tender, 5–6 minutes. Drain.
2 Place in a bowl and gradually add the cream: the mixture should not be too runny. Stir in the parsley, mix well, and season.
3 Preheat the oven to 200°C/400°F/gas 6. Cut a sheet of filo pastry in half lengthwise and arrange one piece on top of the other in a cross shape. Place one-eighth of the filling in the centre and fold over the 4 flaps to make a parcel. Brush with melted butter and place on a baking sheet. Repeat to make 8 parcels.
4 Bake the parcels until golden and crisp: after 20 minutes, turn them over and bake for another 10–15 minutes. Tie with a strip of leek to garnish, if liked. Serve at once.

55 LEEK & SESAME FLAN
Serves 4–6

Ingredients
175g (6oz) prepared shortcrust pastry
self-raising flour, for dusting
30g (1oz) butter, plus extra for greasing
250g (8oz) leeks, sliced
2 tbsp sesame seeds
Savoury custard
3 egg yolks
200ml (7fl oz) single cream
salt and pepper

Serve the flan cut in wedges

1 Roll out the pastry on a lightly floured surface and use to line a 20cm (8in) greased flan tin. Line the pastry case with foil and baking beans and bake blind as described in Tip 21. Remove foil and beans.
2 Melt the butter in a frying pan. Add the leeks, cover, and cook slowly over medium heat, stirring occasionally, until tender, about 15 minutes. If the leeks produce a lot of liquid, uncover, raise the heat, and boil quickly to reduce.
3 To make the custard, beat the egg yolks and cream in a small bowl and season well. Pour into a small pan and cook over gentle heat, stirring continuously with a wooden spoon, until the custard is thick enough to coat the back of the spoon.
4 Preheat the oven to 160°C/ 325°F/gas 3. Arrange the leeks in the flan case and pour on the custard. Sprinkle the sesame seeds over the custard and bake until the filling is set and golden brown on top, 25–30 minutes.

56 SLICING ONIONS
Trim the onion, removing the root. Cut in half from the stem end to the root end. Lay flat side down on a board. Cut in thick or thin slices as required, from root to tip, keeping the root intact. Turn the onion and slice again, cutting at right angles to the first cuts.

Cut lengthwise from stem to root

57 FRENCH ONION SOUP
Serves 6

Ingredients
90g (3oz) butter
1kg (2lb) Spanish onions,
thinly sliced
salt and pepper
1.5 litres (2½ pints)
vegetable stock
2 tsp sugar
250ml (8fl oz) red wine
12 slices French bread
90g (3oz) Gruyère, grated

Float two cheese-topped bread slices on each bowl of soup before serving.

1 Melt 60g (2oz) of the butter in a large pan. Add the onions and season. Cover and cook over low heat until soft but not coloured, about 20 minutes. Meanwhile, boil the stock until it has reduced by one-third, to concentrate its flavour.

2 Sprinkle the onions with the sugar. Cook over medium heat, stirring occasionally, until they are golden brown, 10–12 minutes. Add the stock and the wine. Bring to the boil, then partially cover and simmer for 30 minutes.

3 Preheat the oven to 180°C/350°F/gas 4. Melt the remaining butter and brush the bread on both sides. Place on a baking sheet and bake until lightly browned. Sprinkle with Gruyère and bake until golden brown and crisp.

58 RED ONION & GORGONZOLA PIZZAS
Makes 6

. Ingredients
1½ tsp dried yeast
250ml (8fl oz) warm water
250g (8oz) strong white
(bread) flour, plus extra
75g (2½oz) polenta (fine
cornmeal), plus extra for
sprinkling
salt and pepper
3 tbsp olive oil
Topping
750g (1½lb) red onions
2 tbsp olive oil
2 tsp sugar
4 tbsp red wine
3 tbsp chopped oregano
175g (6oz) Gorgonzola

1 △ Dissolve the yeast in 4 tbsp water. Sift the flour onto a work surface with the polenta and 1 tsp salt. Make a well in the centre; add the remaining water, 2 tbsp oil, and yeast. Gradually draw in the flour with your fingers.

2 △ Form into a soft dough, adding more flour if too sticky. Knead on a floured board until smooth and springy, about 10 minutes. Place in an oiled bowl, cover, and leave in a warm place until doubled in bulk, about 2 hours.

3 △ Slice the onions. Heat oil in a frying pan, add onions and sugar; season. Cook gently until soft, 5–7 minutes. Add the wine and cook for 1 minute, then lower the heat and cover with foil, then a lid. Cook over very low heat for 20 minutes. Stir the oregano into the onions. Preheat oven to 230°C/450°F/gas 8. Cut 6 x 23cm (9in) squares of foil and sprinkle with polenta.

4 △ Knock back dough, then divide into 6 pieces. Roll into 18cm (6in) rounds. Place rounds on foil, forming a rim, and spread with onions. Top with cheese and leave to rise for 15 minutes. Bake on the foil until brown and crisp.

59 PEELING & CHOPPING GARLIC

The strength of garlic varies with its age and dryness. The flavour is milder when it is very young.

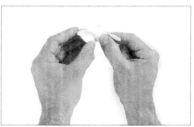

1 △ Separate the bulb into cloves. Crush the cloves lightly with the flat of a heavy knife, then peel off the skin.

2 △ Crush the peeled clove with the flat of the knife, then chop finely, rocking the knife blade back and forth.

60 ROASTING GARLIC

Roasted garlic purée adds a wonderful flavour to sauces, soups, and marinades. Roast whole bulbs in the oven at 180°C/350°F/gas 4 or on a barbecue until tender. Squeeze the flesh from each clove with the back of a knife and purée.

SQUASHES & GOURDS

61 SQUASH & GOURD VARIETIES

These range from large marrows and pumpkins, to small courgettes and squashes. Summer varieties of squash, such as patty-pan, are soft-skinned; winter varieties like butternut are hard-skinned. All contain vitamin A.

◁ *Courgette flowers can be stuffed or deep-fried in batter.*

△ *Pumpkin has fragrant flesh to use in soups, pies, stews, and breads.*

△ *Acorn squash is one of the winter varieties.*

◁ *Cucumbers are often pickled with spices when small.*

△ *Patty-pan are small summer squash with a delicate flavour.*

▽ *Spaghetti squash separates into strands when baked.*

△ *Vegetable marrow is usually stuffed with a herby, minced meat mixture and baked slowly.*

△ *Butternut squash is a hard-skinned winter squash, that must be peeled and deseeded.*

DISCARD PUMPKIN SEEDS

62 PREPARING PUMPKIN

Before peeling and deseeding, cut pumpkins and other varieties of large winter squash into manageable pieces. Scoop out the seeds with a large spoon, and also scrape out the bitter stringy fibres surrounding them.

63 PUMPKIN BREAD

Makes 2 loaves

Ingredients

melted butter, for tins
375g (12oz) strong white
flour, plus extra
2 tsp baking powder
1 tsp salt
2 tsp ground cinnamon
½ tsp ground nutmeg
375ml (12fl oz) pumpkin
purée
125g (4oz) chopped walnuts
3 eggs, beaten
125ml (4fl oz) vegetable oil
200g (7oz) caster sugar
100g (3½oz) brown sugar

1 Preheat the oven to 180°C/350°F/ gas 4. Brush two 20 x 10cm (8 x 4in) loaf tins with melted butter and sprinkle with flour. Turn over and tap to remove excess flour.
2 Sift the flour, baking powder, salt, cinnamon, and nutmeg into a bowl and make a well in the centre. Mix the pumpkin, walnuts, eggs, oil, and sugars, and pour three-quarters of

the mixture into the well.
3 Mix with a spatula, then stir in the remaining pumpkin mixture to make a smooth batter.
4 Pour into the tins and bake until the loaves begin to shrink from the sides and a metal skewer comes out clean, 55–60 minutes.
5 Cool slightly, then turn out onto a wire rack to cool completely.

64 COURGETTE & CARROT RIBBONS

Serves 4

Ingredients
250g (8oz) large carrots
250g (8oz) medium-sized courgettes
salt and pepper
Pesto
1 garlic clove, crushed
15g (½oz) pine nuts
3 tbsp chopped basil leaves
2 tbsp grated Parmesan
3 tbsp olive oil

AN IDEAL SUMMERY DISH

1 To make the pesto, place the ingredients in a food processor and process to a thick green cream.
2 Cut the carrots and courgettes into long, fine strands or ribbons by drawing a swivel-bladed vegetable peeler down their length.
3 Pour 1cm (½in) of boiling water into a pan and add the carrot ribbons. Cover and cook over a moderate heat for 2–3 minutes. Add the courgette ribbons and cook for another 1–2 minutes. The courgettes cook quickly – don't let them become waterlogged. Remove from the heat and drain thoroughly in a colander.
4 Transfer the courgette and carrot ribbons to a serving dish, add 2 tbsp pesto and season. Toss gently until well coated with the pesto. Serve immediately. Store any remaining pesto in the refrigerator.

65 MAKING COURGETTE BOATS

Courgette boats are ideal for savoury stuffings. Use medium-sized courgettes. Halve lengthwise, then blanch (*Tip 8*) for 3–4 minutes. Scoop out seeds and a little flesh, leaving skin intact. Mix flesh with chosen stuffing and bake for 15 minutes in a moderate oven.

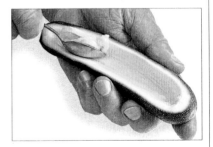

SCOOPING OUT SEEDS

66 STUFFED COURGETTES

Serves 4

Ingredients

4 medium courgettes, halved lengthwise
2 tbsp olive oil
1 onion, chopped
2 red peppers, cored, deseeded, and diced
2 large garlic cloves, chopped
2 tbsp chopped fresh thyme
45g (1½oz) flaked almonds, toasted briefly
salt and pepper

1 Preheat the oven to 180°C/ 350°F/ gas 4. Blanch the courgettes in boiling water for 3–4 minutes (*Tip 8*). Drain and cool. Scoop out seeds and a little flesh, and reserve. Place courgettes in a greased dish.
2 Warm oil in a small pan. Add onion and red pepper, cover, and cook until soft. Add garlic, thyme, reserved flesh, and almonds, and season. Spoon into the courgette halves and bake for 15 minutes.

67 PREPARING MARROW

This works well for marrow and other large squashes with tough seeds. Trim end and cut vegetable into thick rings. Scoop out seeds and stringy fibres with a teaspoon.

ALWAYS REMOVE SEEDS BEFORE COOKING

68 PICKLED GHERKINS

Mix 1kg (2lb) gherkins with 250g (8oz) coarse salt and leave for 24 hours. Drain, rinse thoroughly in a large bowl of water, and drain again. Wipe dry on paper towels, then place in 2 sterilized glass preserving jars. Add 60g (2oz) pickling onions, 3 dried chillies, 3 sprigs thyme, 1 bay leaf, 2 sprigs tarragon, and 3 cloves to each jar. Fill the jars with white wine vinegar, seal, and store in the refrigerator for 4 weeks before eating. Use within 3 months.

ROOT VEGETABLES

69 ROOT VARIETIES

Roots include more unusual vegetables like scorzonera, daikon, and celeriac, as well as the more familiar carrots and turnips. They are a good source of carbohydrates, fibre, and vitamin C. Unlike green vegetables, roots start cooking in cold water, and are simmered, not boiled.

△ **Swedes** are best in winter, before they become too fibrous.

▽ **Turnips** are best young, when they have a sweet, nutty flavour, and the tops have a peppery taste.

△ **Beetroot** is available fresh all year. Try it hot, with melted butter.

▽ **Celeriac** has a sweet flavour, like mild celery. Avoid large, woody specimens.

▷ **Scorzonera,** and its relative salsify, have a delicate flavour.

◁ **Daikon** (Japanese radish) has less bite than other radishes.

▷ **Parsnips** have a high natural sugar content and combine sweetness with nuttiness.

70 GLAZING ROOTS

Vegetables such as carrots or turnips are delicious glazed. Cook a selection separately, but serve together. Place 500g (1lb) in a pan with 45g (1½oz) butter, 1 tbsp sugar, and enough water to barely cover. Simmer until the liquid has almost evaporated, then shake pan to coat vegetables with the glaze.

AN ASSORTMENT OF GLAZED VEGETABLES

71 CARROT FLAN WITH CARDAMOM

Makes 6–8

Ingredients

175g (6oz) shortcrust pastry
plain flour, for dusting
125g (4oz) baby carrots, finely
sliced crosswise
1 whole green cardamom pod
1 egg
125ml (4fl oz) single cream
salt and black pepper

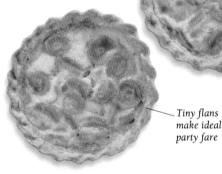

Tiny flans make ideal party fare

1 Roll out the pastry on a lightly floured surface and line 6–8 7cm (3in) tartlet cases. Line the cases with foil and baking beans, and bake blind as described in Tip 21.
2 Preheat the oven to 160°C/325°F/gas 3. Place the carrots in a pan with the cardamom pod and enough water to cover. Bring to the boil, and cook until tender, about 2 minutes. Drain the carrots thoroughly and divide them evenly among the pastry cases.
3 Split the cardamom pod, scoop out the seeds, and mix in a bowl with the egg and cream. Season to taste. Fill the cases with the cardamom mixture and bake until the filling is set, 5–10 minutes. Serve warm or cold.

Test with tip of knife

72 BOILING & SKINNING BEETROOT

Trim and scrub beetroot, then place in a pan and just cover with salted water. Bring to the boil and cook until tender when tested with a knife, about 30 minutes. Drain well, and skin when cool enough to handle. Never skin beetroot before cooking as the colour bleeds.

73 BORSCHT

Serves 8–10

Ingredients

1kg (2lb) beetroot
1.4kg (3lb) white cabbage
60g (2oz) butter
2 carrots, diced
2 onions, diced
750g (1½lb) tomatoes, skinned, deseeded, and chopped
2 litres (3¼ pints) chicken stock, plus extra if needed
1 tsp sugar
salt and pepper
4 dill sprigs, chopped
4 parsley sprigs, chopped
juice of 1 lemon
2–3 tbsp wine vinegar
125ml (4fl oz) sour cream

COOKING AHEAD
Borscht can be stored in the refrigerator for 2–3 days: the flavour will improve. It can also be frozen for up to 3 months.

1 Boil and skin the beetroot (*Tip 72*). Grate the beetroot onto a plate. Cut the cabbage in half and cut out the core. Shred each half finely, discarding any thick ribs.
2 Melt the butter in a large pan, add the carrots and onions, and cook gently until soft but not brown, 3–5 minutes.
2 Add the cabbage, beetroot, tomatoes, stock, and sugar to the pan. Season, then bring to the boil. Simmer for 45–60 minutes, taste for seasoning, and add more stock if it is too thick.
3 Stir in the chopped herbs, lemon juice, and vinegar, and taste for seasoning. Pour the soup into a warmed tureen and top with sour cream.

74 BEETROOT & CELERIAC SALAD
Serves 6

Ingredients
3 tbsp cider vinegar
1 tsp sugar
2 tsp caraway seeds
salt and pepper
75ml (2½fl oz) vegetable oil
500g (1lb) beetroot
750g (1½lb) celeriac
175ml (6fl oz) mayonnaise
2 tbsp horseradish sauce

1 Make the dressing by whisking together the vinegar, sugar, caraway seeds, salt, pepper, and oil in a bowl until thickened. Boil and skin the beetroot (*Tip 72*) and grate coarsely.

2 Add the grated beetroot to the dressing, toss gently, and taste for seasoning. Cover and chill for 1 hour. Peel the celeriac, cut thinly in vertical slices, then cut into very fine, even strips.

3 Place the mayonnaise and horseradish in a bowl and season. Add the celeriac, toss well, then cover and chill for 1 hour. To serve, arrange in alternate stripes on a serving dish.

75 CELERIAC PURÉE
Peel 500g (1lb) celeriac and 250g (8oz) potatoes. Cut into chunks and cook in boiling water until tender. Drain, add 15g (½oz) butter and mash with a potato masher, softening with a little milk or cream, if liked. Season to taste.

76 ROASTED ROOT VEGETABLES
Cut 750g (1½lb) each potatoes, parsnips, celeriac, and carrots into chunks and place in a roasting tin with 6 tbsp olive oil. Turn to coat and cook in a hot oven for about 40 minutes until tender and crisp.

TUBERS

77 TUBER VARIETIES

Tubers are a good source of minerals and B group vitamins. Many of these nutrients are in or just beneath the skin, but pesticides and other chemical residues also gather in the skin, so it is safest to peel these vegetables before eating, unless organically grown.

△ *Baking potatoes can be enjoyed with their skin on, if organically grown.*

▷ **White potatoes** *can be creamy, floury, or waxy in texture, depending on variety.*

▷ **Jerusalem artichokes** *have a nutty flavour. Look for ones that are not too knobbly.*

▷ **White sweet potatoes** *can be boiled, baked, puréed, or served as deep-fried chips.*

◁ **Red sweet potatoes** *are good with roasts, or mashed and used in soufflés or stuffings.*

◁ **Yams** *are high in starch. They can be cooked in the same way as ordinary potatoes.*

◁ **Red potatoes** *can be waxy or floury in texture. Firm varieties that hold their shape are ideal for salads.*

78 JERUSALEM ARTICHOKE SOUP

Warm 1 tbsp olive oil in a large pan, add 1 chopped onion, cover, and cook for 5 minutes. Add 500g (1lb) Jerusalem artichokes, peeled, diced, and tossed in lemon juice to prevent discoloration. Stir well, cover, and cook for 5–10 minutes. Add 1 litre (1¾ pints) vegetable stock, bring to the boil, then cook gently until tender, about 15 minutes. Liquidize the soup in a food processor, then return to the pan and reheat. Season with salt, pepper, and nutmeg. Stir in 150ml (¼ pint) cream just before serving.

79 USING A MANDOLIN

A mandolin has an adjustable blade for slicing wafer-thin rounds of vegetables. It is particularly useful for obtaining different shapes of potato for deep-frying (*Tip 80*).

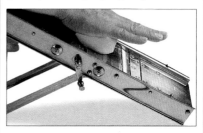

ADJUST BLADE FOR THICKNESS

80 DEEP-FRIED POTATOES SIX DIFFERENT WAYS

 The potato pieces should always be of uniform thickness and size. Keep them in water to avoid discoloration and to soak out some starch. Dry thoroughly on paper towels, then fry at 190°C/375°F.

△ FRENCH FRIED (4–5 MINS)

△ SOUFFLÉD (4–5 MINS)

△ STRAW (2–3 MINS)

△ WAFFLED (2–3 MINS)

△ CRISPS (2–3 MINS)

△ MATCHSTICK (3–4 MINS)

81 PERFECT MASHED POTATOES

Use floury or baking potatoes: peel and boil, then drain well. Mash with a potato masher or work with a mouli, but do not use a food processor, as this makes them gluey. For 750g (1½lb) beat in about 125–175ml (4–6fl oz) hot milk until the texture is light and fluffy, then beat in 90g (3oz) butter and season well.

USE A POTATO MASHER

82 SPICED POTATOES

Serves 4

Ingredients
2 tbsp groundnut oil
1 onion, chopped
2 garlic cloves, chopped
2 tsp ground cumin
2 tsp ground coriander
½ tsp turmeric
¼ tsp cayenne pepper
750g (1½lb) waxy
potatoes, peeled and diced
salt and pepper
1 tsp garam masala
2–4 tbsp chopped
coriander leaves

1 Warm the oil in a pan over medium heat, add the onion, cover and cook for 5 minutes until soft.
2 Add the garlic, cumin, ground coriander, turmeric, and cayenne and cook for 2 minutes, stirring.
3 Add the potatoes and stir until they are well coated with the onion and spices. Add 1 tsp salt and 150ml (5oz) water, bring to the boil, then cover and cook over gentle heat until just tender and most of the water has been absorbed, about 10–15 minutes.
3 Stir in the garam masala. Season to taste and add more cayenne if liked. Serve the potatoes warm or cool, sprinkled with coriander.

83 SPINACH & POTATO GNOCCHI
Serves 8

Ingredients
1kg (2lb) potatoes, peeled
250g (8oz) fresh spinach
125g (4oz) plain flour,
plus extra for dusting
Tomato cream sauce
45g (1½oz) butter, plus
extra for greasing
1 small onion, diced
1 carrot, diced
1 celery stick, diced
1.4kg (3lb) tomatoes,
peeled and deseeded
salt and pepper
250ml (8fl oz) double
cream
1 tbsp chopped parsley

1 △ To make the sauce, melt butter in a frying pan, add onion, carrot, and celery and cook until tender, about 10 minutes. Chop the tomatoes, add to the pan, season, and simmer, stirring until thick, 25–35 minutes. Purée in a food processor.

2 △ Boil the potatoes until tender. Drain well, return to the pan to dry, then mash. Cook the spinach in boiling water for 2 minutes. Drain and squeeze dry, then chop finely. Mix into the potatoes with the flour to form a dough, and season.

4 ◁ Preheat the oven to 220°C/425°F/gas 7. Reheat sauce, stir in the cream, and season. Spoon over the gnocchi. Bake for 5–7 minutes. Garnish with chopped parsley.

3 △ Knead the dough on a floured board to bind well. Divide into 12 pieces and roll each piece into a long cylinder. Cut crosswise into 2cm (¾in) pieces. Boil the gnocchi in batches for 2 minutes, drain well, and place in a greased baking dish.

84 VEGETABLES AU GRATIN

Au gratin means that cooked
vegetables are coated with a cheese
or béchamel sauce, then baked in a
shallow dish sprinkled with grated
cheese or breadcrumbs. The gratin
is baked until golden, and can then
be browned under the grill.

Top with cheese or crumbs

85 POTATO GRATIN
Serves 8

Ingredients
750g (1½lb) waxy potatoes
600ml (1 pint) milk
pinch of ground nutmeg
salt and pepper
300ml (½ pint) double cream
45g (1½oz) Gruyère, grated
1 garlic clove, halved
melted butter, for greasing

1 Cut the potatoes into
3mm (⅛in) slices.
Bring the milk to the boil
in a large pan, add the
nutmeg, and season. Add
the potatoes and cook for
10 minutes.

2 Drain, return to the
pan, and add the
cream. Simmer gently for
10–15 minutes. Rub a
shallow baking dish with
the cut garlic and brush
with melted butter.

3 Preheat the oven to
190°C/375°F/gas 5.
Layer the potatoes and
cream in the dish and
sprinkle with the cheese.
Bake until golden brown
on top, 20–25 minutes.

SHOOT VEGETABLES

86 SHOOT VARIETIES

Shoots are high in fibre. They have a juicy crispness and usually need only brief cooking. They often discolour easily after cutting. If not used immediately after preparation, put in water to cover with lemon juice, until ready to cook.

▷ *Chicory has a plump white head. Cooking mellows its bitter flavour.*

▷ *Globe artichokes can be boiled whole or stuffed and baked.*

◁ *Celery is best cooked braised. It is often used to flavour soups and stews.*

▷ *Jumbo asparagus has large stems that need to be peeled before cooking.*

△ *Fennel bulbs have a slight aniseed flavour. They can be baked or roasted.*

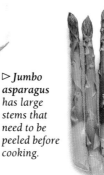

▷ *White asparagus is picked before it has sprouted above ground.*

87 PREPARING ASPARAGUS

Using a vegetable peeler, peel off the tough outer skin at the bottom of each asparagus stalk, working from the tip of the stalk towards the base. Trim off the woody ends, if necessary. If the asparagus is young and slender, it may not need peeling. Tie the stalks into bundles with kitchen string, ready for boiling.

PEEL OFF TOUGH SKIN

88 ASPARAGUS FILO FLOWERS

Serves 4

Ingredients
1–2 sheets filo pastry
melted butter, for brushing
24 asparagus tips
Hollandaise sauce
2 tbsp white wine vinegar
250g (8oz) butter
2 large egg yolks
salt and pepper

Arrange filo squares so they overlap

1 To make the sauce, place the vinegar in a small pan with 3 tbsp of water and boil until reduced to 1 tbsp. Allow to cool. Melt the butter in a small pan. Place the egg yolks and vinegar in a blender and blend until well combined. With the machine running, slowly pour in the butter. As it thickens, add the butter more quickly. Season and keep warm over hot water.
2 Preheat the oven to 200°C/400°F/gas 6. Take a 12-hole bun tin. Cut 2 squares of filo pastry for each hole, but slightly larger. Brush each hole with butter, put in one square of pastry, then another at a crosswise angle. Brush again. Bake until golden and crisp, about 5 minutes. Leave to cool.
3 Boil the asparagus until tender; cool. Place the filo flowers on a plate, fill with the sauce and arrange 2 asparagus tips on each.

FILO PASTRY
Filo pastry dries out quickly and becomes brittle, so remove one sheet at a time, and keep the rest covered with clingfilm or a damp cloth until needed.

89 ASPARAGUS ROULADE

Serves 6

Ingredients

*butter & dry grated
Parmesan to coat the tin
175g (6oz) curd cheese
150ml (5fl oz) single cream
4 eggs, separated
200g (7oz) Gruyère
3 tbsp mixed chopped
chervil & flat-leaf parsley
salt and pepper
400g (14oz) asparagus tips*

ROLLING A ROULADE
*Start from a short side.
Use the nonstick paper
underneath to help lift
the base as you roll.
Place the roulade on a
plate or board with the
seam underneath
so it cannot
unroll.*

1 Preheat the oven to 200°C/400°F/gas 6. Line a 22 x 32cm (9 x 13in) Swiss roll tin with nonstick paper, butter, and dust with Parmesan.
2 Beat 60g (2oz) curd cheese in a bowl with the cream until smooth. Beat in the egg yolks one by one. Stir in the Gruyère and herbs. Season.
3 Whisk the egg whites until stiff and fold into the cheese mixture with a metal spoon. Pour into the Swiss roll tin, smooth the top, and bake until risen and just firm and springy in the centre. Turn out onto nonstick paper sprinkled with Parmesan and peel off the lining paper.
4 Steam the asparagus until tender. Soften the remaining curd cheese with a little water and spread over the roulade. Arrange the asparagus in rows, starting from a short side. Roll up from a short side and serve at once, cut into slices.

90 ROASTED FENNEL OR CHICORY

Preheat the oven to 230°C/450°F/gas 8. Trim feathery fennel tops, and cut the bulbs into quarters lengthways. Leave chicory whole, but trim the root end. Put vegetables in a roasting tin, brush with olive oil; roast for 20 minutes. Reduce temperature to 180°C/350°F/gas 4, turn the vegetables, brush again with oil, and roast 15–20 minutes more until slightly browned and tender. Season. Serve hot or warm.

CUT LENGTHWAYS

91 PREPARING GLOBE ARTICHOKES

Artichokes can be boiled until tender, 30–45 minutes, and served whole with melted butter or a sauce. Alternatively, the choke and internal leaves can be removed before or after cooking, and a sauce or stuffing spooned in.

1 ▷ Snap off the stem from each artichoke so that the fibres are pulled out with the stalk. Grip the stem firmly so that it snaps cleanly and sharply.

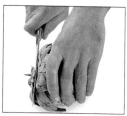

2 △ Using a heavy sharp knife, trim the base of each artichoke so that it sits flat. Rub cut surfaces with lemon juice.

3 △ Trim the tough outer leaves of the artichoke with kitchen scissors to remove the pointed tips.

4 △ Using a heavy knife, cut off the top of each artichoke, parallel to the base. Rub with lemon juice.

92 ROMAN-STYLE ARTICHOKES
Serves 6

Ingredients
6 young globe artichokes
3 lemons, 1 sliced and 2 halved
10 sprigs fresh mint
6 garlic cloves, finely chopped
1 bunch flat-leaf parsley, finely chopped
salt and pepper
125ml (4fl oz) olive oil

1 △ Prepare the artichokes (*Tip 91*) and peel the stems. Hollow out centres and scoop out chokes. Rub inside and out with 3 of the lemon halves. Chop 8 mint sprigs. Mix garlic, parsley, and chopped mint to make the stuffing. Season.

2 △ Place 2–3 tsp of stuffing in each artichoke. Set artichokes in a large pan, stems up. Sprinkle with remaining stuffing and oil. Season. Add water to come halfway up. Bring to the boil. Cover and simmer 30–45 minutes until tender.

3 △ Transfer artichokes to serving dish and boil liquid to reduce to 250ml (8fl oz). Add juice of remaining ½ lemon to pan, then pour over artichokes. Garnish with lemon slices and mint sprigs.

93 STUFFED ARTICHOKES
Serves 4

Ingredients

4 large globe artichokes
½ lemon
45g (1½oz) butter
3 onions, finely chopped
6 garlic cloves, finely chopped
250g (8oz) mushrooms, finely chopped
250g (8oz) Parma ham, chopped
2 anchovy fillets, finely chopped
175g (6oz) stoned black olives, chopped
salt and pepper

4 slices white bread
2–3 sprigs thyme, leaves chopped
pinch of ground allspice
250ml (8fl oz) white wine
Red pepper sauce
750g (1½lb) red peppers
2 tbsp olive oil
500g (1lb) tomatoes, peeled and chopped
1 garlic clove, chopped
2 spring onions, chopped
3 tbsp chopped basil, plus 4 sprigs

1 △ Prepare the artichokes (Tip 91) and rub the cut surfaces with the lemon half. Place in a large pan of boiling salted water and cook until almost tender and a leaf can be pulled out, 25–30 minutes. Drain upside down until cool, then remove inner leaves and scoop out chokes with a teaspoon.

2 △ To make the stuffing, melt the butter in a frying pan, add the onions and garlic, and cook until soft but not brown. Add the mushrooms, ham, anchovies, and olives, then remove from the heat. Season. Work the bread into crumbs in a food processor. Mix in with the thyme and allspice.

3 △ Preheat the oven to 180°C/350°F/ gas 4. Spoon the stuffing into the artichokes and tie each one with string to hold the leaves together. Place in a casserole and pour in the wine. Boil until wine is reduced by half, then add enough water to come halfway up.

5 △ For the sauce, grill and deseed the peppers (*Tip 38*); cut into chunks. Heat the olive oil in a frying pan. Add the peppers, tomatoes, garlic, spring onions, and chopped basil. Cook until thick, stirring. Purée briefly in a food processor until barely chunky. Season.

4 △ Cover, bring back to a boil, then cook in the oven until tender and a leaf can be pulled out easily, 40–50 minutes, basting occasionally. Add more hot water if necessary. Before serving, remove the strings. Garnish with basil sprigs and accompany with red pepper sauce (*Step 5, above right*).

MUSHROOMS

94 CULTIVATED VARIETIES

Mushrooms give dishes a rich, earthy flavour and chewy texture, and are high in vitamins A and D. They deteriorate quickly if too moist. Do not wrap in plastic, but store, loosely wrapped in paper or in a brown paper bag, in the refrigerator for 3–4 days.

▷ *Shiitake is a Chinese variety with an intense flavour.*

◁ *Oyster mushrooms have a mild flavour and chewy texture.*

▷ *Common mushrooms are flat when more mature.*

◁ *Cultivated mushrooms are available as buttons or caps, open or closed.*

95 WILD VARIETIES

These have a much stronger, more distinctive flavour than the cultivated varieties. Some can now be found, in season, in specialist shops. If gathering them yourself, eat only after they have been checked by an expert, as poisonous varieties are often almost identical to edible ones.

▷ *Chanterelles are favoured for their fine aroma and perfumed taste.*

◁ *Chicken of the woods are best when moist and springy. They make good soup and stir-fries.*

▷ *Boletus (also known as ceps or porcini) have a flavour that is both pungent and perfumed. They are also available dried.*

96 TRUFFLES

Truffles grow only near the roots of oak trees, and are gathered during autumn. Fresh truffles are greatly prized for their flavour and aroma (which is highly distinctive), but are expensive and often hard to find. Their incomparable quality is best savoured by grating them into simple salads, pasta, and egg dishes such as omelettes, although their intensity of flavour also comes through in stuffings and pâtés.

◁ *Périgord (French) black truffles, with an almost overwhelming aroma, are the most highly sought after.*

◁ *Piedmontese (Italian) white truffles are spicily reminiscent of pepper in both aroma and flavour.*

97 PREPARING MUSHROOMS

Pick over mushrooms and trim the stalks, cutting off any woody parts from wild mushrooms. There is no need to peel them. Wipe or brush off any earth with a damp cloth, but avoid washing mushrooms as they easily become waterlogged. If they are sandy, rinse very quickly and drain well in a colander.

98 GREEK-STYLE MUSHROOMS

Serves 4

Ingredients
3 tbsp olive oil
20 baby or pickling onions
125ml (4fl oz) white wine
300ml (½ pint) chicken stock
250g (8oz) tomatoes, peeled and chopped
1 tbsp tomato purée
juice of ½ lemon
1 tbsp black peppercorns
2 tbsp coriander seeds
½ tsp dried thyme
salt and pepper
750g (1½lb) small mushrooms

1 Heat the oil in a pan, add the onions, and cook for 2–3 minutes. Add all the remaining ingredients, except the mushrooms, and bring to the boil. Add the mushrooms and cook over high heat for 15–20 minutes until the liquid is reduced. **2** Leave to cool, then season to taste. Chill before serving.

99 STUFFED SHIITAKE
Serves 4

Ingredients
350g (12oz) medium or large shiitake
60g (2oz) butter, plus extra for greasing
1 onion, finely chopped
1 tbsp lemon juice
125g (4oz) chopped ham
60g (2oz) white breadcrumbs
2 tbsp chopped parsley
salt and pepper

1 Preheat the oven to 180°C/
350°F/gas 4. Cut off the shiitake
stalks and chop with 2 of the caps.
2 Melt the butter in a frying pan
and fry the onion until soft. Stir in
the mushrooms and lemon juice
and cook for 3–5 minutes.
3 Remove from the heat and stir
in the ham, breadcrumbs, and
parsley. Season. Pile the stuffing
into the mushroom caps and place
in a buttered baking dish. Bake
until tender, 10–15 minutes.

100 MIXED WILD MUSHROOMS
Serves 4

Ingredients
125g (4oz) frisée, leaves torn
1 small head of radicchio, leaves
separated
75g (2½oz) rocket, trimmed
375g (12oz) wild mushrooms, such as
chanterelles, ceps and oyster mushrooms
45g (1½oz) butter
2 shallots, diced
1 small bunch parsley, finely chopped
vinaigrette dressing

1 Mix the salad leaves with the
rocket. Trim mushroom stalks and
remove any woody stems. Cut the
mushrooms into even-sized pieces.
2 Heat the butter in a frying pan.
Add the shallots and cook until soft,
2–3 minutes. Add mushrooms.
Cook, stirring, until mushrooms
are tender and the liquid has
evaporated. Stir in the parsley.
3 Toss the leaves with the
vinaigrette. Arrange on 4 plates
and top with the mushrooms.

101 BAKED POLENTA WITH WILD MUSHROOMS
Serves 4

Ingredients
1.5 litres (2½ pints) water
1 tbsp salt
275g (12oz) polenta (cornmeal)
3 tbsp olive oil, plus extra
250g (8oz) wild mushrooms,
woody stems trimmed, chopped
3 garlic cloves, finely chopped
3 sprigs thyme, leaves chopped
125ml (4fl oz) dry white wine
250ml (8fl oz) vegetable stock
4 tbsp double cream
salt and pepper
250g (8oz) Fontina cheese, sliced

1 Sprinkle 2 baking sheets with water. Bring the water and salt to the boil in a large pan. Slowly pour in the polenta over medium heat, whisking constantly to avoid lumps. Cook for 10–15 minutes, stirring, until smooth and soft. Spread evenly over the baking sheets and chill.

2 Heat the oil in a frying pan. Add the mushrooms, garlic, and thyme, and cook until tender and the liquid has evaporated, 7 minutes. Add the wine and simmer for 2–3 minutes. Add the stock and cook until it is reduced by half. Stir in the cream until mixture thickens slightly. Season.

3 Preheat the oven to 220°C/425°F/gas 7. Cut polenta into squares, trim to fit, and arrange half in an oiled dish. Cover with half the mushrooms and place half the cheese on top. Add remaining mushrooms; top with the polenta trimmings and cheese. Bake 20–25 minutes.

INDEX

ACKNOWLEDGMENTS

Dorling Kindersley would like to thank Hilary Bird for compiling the index, Fiona Wild for proof-reading, Richard Hammond for editorial help, and Robert Campbell for DTP assistance.

Photography
All photographs by Martin Brigdale, Philip Dowell, Amanda Heywood, Dave King, David Murray, Stephen Oliver, Jules Selmes, Clive Streeter, and Jerry Young.

Additional recipes by Anne Willan
Tip 13 *Mixed vegetable curry*; Tip 14 *Thai-style stir-fried vegetables*; Tip 21 *Broccoli & mushroom quiche*; Tip 27 *Chestnut-stuffed cabbage*; Tip 29 *Swiss chard crêpes*; Tip 31 *Spinach timbales*; Tip 57 *French onion soup*; Tip 58 *Red onion & Gorgonzola pizzas*; Tip 63 *Pumpkin bread*; Tip 73 *Borscht*; Tip 74 *Beetroot & celeriac salad*; Tip 83 *Spinach & potato gnocchi*; Tip 85 *Potato gratin*; Tip 92 *Roman-style artichokes*; Tip 93 *Stuffed artichokes*; Tip 98 *Greek-style mushrooms*; Tip 99 *Stuffed shiitake*; Tip 100 *Mixed wild mushrooms*; Tip 101 *Baked polenta with wild mushrooms*.